Texts for Fluency Practice

Level B

Authors

Timothy Rasinski and Lorraine Griffith

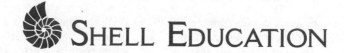

SHELL EDUCATION

Editor
Tracy Edmunds

Imaging
Alfred Lau

Product Director
Phil Garcia

Cover Design
Lee Aucoin

Creative Director
Lee Aucoin

Editor-in-Chief
Sharon Coan, M.S. Ed.

Publisher
Corinne Burton, M.A.ED.

Shell Education

5301 Oceanus Drive
Huntington Beach, CA 92649-1030

http://www.shelleducation.com
ISBN 978-1-4258-0399-5

©2005 Shell Education
Reprinted 2010
Made in U.S.A.

Table of Contents

Table of Contents

Introduction

Why This Book?

We developed this book in response to teachers' needs for good texts to teach reading fluency. In the past several years, reading fluency has become recognized as an essential element in elementary and middle grade reading programs (National Reading Panel, 2001). Readers who are fluent are better able to comprehend what they read—they decode words so effortlessly that they can devote their cognitive resources to the all-important task of comprehension. Fluent readers also construct meaning by reading with appropriate expression and phrasing.

Readers develop fluency through guided practice or repeated readings— reading a text selection several times to the point where it can be expressed meaningfully, with appropriate expression and phrasing. Readers who engage in regular repeated readings, under the guidance and assistance of a teacher or other coach, improve their word recognition, reading rate, comprehension, and overall reading proficiency.

What sorts of texts lend themselves to repeated practice? To us, texts meant to be performed or read orally for an audience are ideal texts for guided repeated reading and reading fluency development. Our goal in this book has been to collect age-appropriate texts meant to be performed or read aloud by students. We have found texts that are relatively short so they can be read and reread in brief periods of time. These texts are from a variety of genres—poetry and rhymes; song lyrics; famous speeches and quotations; Reader's Theater Scripts; and other texts such as jokes, cheers, and well wishes. These delightful texts are often neglected in the regular reading program that focuses largely on narrative and informational texts. The passages in this book are also part of our cultural heritage and are important parts of the cultural literacy curriculum for elementary students. Even if you are not teaching reading fluency, your students should read the texts in this book as part of their cultural heritage.

Students will find the texts in this book enjoyable and engaging. They will want to practice reading these texts because of their engaging qualities—the language patterns, the rhyme, the melody, and the inspiration they provide. They will especially want to practice the texts if you provide regular opportunities for your students to perform the texts for their classmates, parents, and other audiences.

Have fun with these texts. Read them with your students again and again. Be assured that if your students regularly read and perform the texts in this book they will begin to develop into fluent readers who are able to decode words effortlessly and construct meaning through their oral interpretation of texts.

Introduction *(cont)*

How to Use This Book

The texts in this book are engaging and enjoyable. Students will want to read, reread, and perform these texts. As they do, they will develop into fluent readers, improving their ability to recognize words accurately and effortlessly and reading with meaningful expression and phrasing. However, you, the teacher, are the most important part in developing instruction that uses these texts. In this section we recommend ways you can use the texts with your students.

Scheduling and Practice

The texts need to be read repeatedly over several days. We recommend you introduce one text at a time and practice it over the next three, four, or five days, depending on how quickly your students develop mastery over the texts. Write the text you are going to teach on chart paper and/or put it on an overhead transparency.

Read the text with your students several times each day. Read it a few times at the beginning of each day; read it several times during various breaks in the day; and read it multiple times at the end of each day.

Make two copies of the text for each student Have students keep one copy at school in a "fluency folder." The other copy can be sent home for students to continue practicing the text with their families. Communicate to families the importance of children continuing to practice the text at home with their parents and other family members.

Coaching Your Students

A key ingredient to repeated reading is the coaching that comes from you, the teacher. As your students practice reading the target text each week—alone, in small groups, or as an entire class—be sure to provide positive feedback about their reading. Through oral interpretation of a text readers can express joy, sadness, anger, surprise, or any of a variety of emotions. Help students learn to convey emotion and meaning in their oral reading.

You can do this by listening from time to time to students read and coaching them in the various aspects of oral interpretation. You may wish to suggest that students emphasize certain words, insert dramatic pauses, read a bit faster in one place, or slow down in other parts of the text. And, of course, lavish praise on students' best efforts to convey meaning through their reading. Although it may take a while for students to develop this sense of "voice" in their reading, in the long run it will lead to more engaged and fluent reading and higher levels of comprehension.

Introduction *(cont)*

Word Study

Although the aim of the fluency texts in this book is to develop fluent and meaningful oral reading of texts, the practicing of passages should also provide opportunities to develop students' vocabulary and word decoding skills. Students may practice a passage repeatedly to the point where it is largely memorized. At this point, students may not look at the words in the text as closely as they should. By continually drawing attention to words in the text, you can help students maintain their focus and develop an ongoing fascination with words.

After reading a passage several times through, ask students to choose words from the passage that they think are interesting. Put these words on a word wall or ask students to add them to their personal word banks. Talk about the meaning of each word and its spelling construction. Help students develop a deepened appreciation for these words and encourage them to use these words in their oral and written language. You might, for example, ask students to use some of the chosen words in their daily journal entries.

Once a list of words has been added to your classroom word wall or students' word banks, play games with the words. One of our favorites is "word bingo." Here, students are given a card with a grid of 3 x 3, 4 x 4, or 5 x 5 boxes. In each box students randomly write a word from the word wall or bank. Then, the teacher calls out definitions of the target words or sentences that contain the target words. Students find the words on their cards and cover them with a marker. Once a horizontal, vertical, or diagonal line of words is covered, they call "Bingo" and win the game.

Have students sort the chosen words along a variety of dimensions — by number of syllables, part of speech, phonics features such as long vowel sound or a consonant blend, or by meaning (e.g. words that can express how a person can feel and words that can't). Through sorting and categorizing activities students get repeated exposure to words, all the time examining the words in different ways.

Help students expand their vocabularies with extended word family instruction. Choose a word from the texts, like "hat", and brainstorm with students other words that belong to the same word family (e.g, "cat," "bat," "chat," etc.). Once a list of family words is chosen, have students create short poems using the rhyming words. These composed poems can be used for further practice and performance. No matter how you do it, make the opportunity to examine select words from the fluency passages part of your regular instructional routine for the fluency texts. The time spent in word study will most definitely be time very well spent.

Introduction *(cont)*

Performance

After several days of practice, arrange a special time of a day for students to perform the texts. This performance time can range from 5 minutes to 30 minutes depending on the number of texts to be read. Find a special person to listen to your children perform. You may also want to invite a neighboring class, parents, or another group to come to your room to listen to your students read. Have the children perform the targeted text as a group. Later, you can have individuals or groups of children perform the text again.

As an alternative to having your children perform for a group that comes to your room, you may want to send students to visit other adults and children in the building and perform for them. Principals, school secretaries, and visitors to the building are usually great audiences for children's reading. Tape recording and videotaping your students' reading is another way to create a performance opportunity.

Regardless of how you accomplish it, it is important that you create the opportunity for your students to perform for some audience. The magic of the performance will give students the motivation to want to practice their assigned texts.

Performance, Not Memorization

Remember, the key to developing fluency is guided reading practice. Students become more fluent when they read the text repeatedly. Reading requires students to actually see the words in the text. Thus, it is important that you do not require students to memorize the text they are practicing and performing. Memorization leads students away from the visualization of the words. Although students may want to try to memorize some texts, our instructional emphasis needs to be on reading with expression so that any audience will enjoy the students' oral rendering of the text. Keep students' eyes on the text whenever possible.

Introduction *(cont)*

Reader's Theater

Reader's Theater is an exciting and easy method of providing students with an opportunity to practice fluency leading to a performance. Because Reader's Theater minimizes the use of props, sets, costumes, and memorization, it is an easy way to present a "play" in the classroom. Students read from a book or prepared script using their voices to bring to text to life.

Reader's Theater is a communication form that establishes contact with the audience. In traditional drama, the audience is ignored as they watch the characters perform. Reader's Theater, on the other hand, has the following characteristics:

- The script is always read and never memorized.

- Readers may be characters, narrators, or switch back and forth into various characters and parts.

- The readers may sit, stand, or both, but they do not have to perform any other actions.

- Readers use only the interpreter's tools to express emotion. These are eye contact, facial expressions, and vocal expression. The voice, especially, should be very expressive.

- Scripts may be from books, songs, poems, letters, etc. They can be performed directly from the original material or adapted specifically for the Reader's Theater performance.

- Musical accompaniment or soundtracks may be used, but is not necessary.

- Very simple props may be used, especially with younger children, to help the audience identify the parts.

Practice for the Reader's Theater should consist of coached repeated readings that lead to a smooth, fluent presentation.

Websites and Resources for Fluency and Fluency Texts

http://www.theteachersguide.com/ChildrensSongs.htm — children's songs

http://www.niehs.nih.gov/kids/musicchild.htm — children's songs

http://www.gigglepoetry.com – fun and silly poetry

http://loiswalker.com/catalog/guidesamples.html — various scripts

http://www.ruyasonic.com/rdr_edu.htm — information on writing radio drama scripts

http://www.ruyasonic.com/at_kids.htm — information on writing radio drama scripts for children

http://www.margiepalatini.com/readerstheater.html — Reader's Theater scripts

http://www.aaronshep.com/rt/ — Reader's Theater resource

http://www.storycart.com — Reader's Theater scripts (5 free)

Note: These websites were active at the time of publication. As you know sites frequently change, so we cannot guarantee that they will always be available or at the same location.

Poetry and Rhymes

The New Colossus

By Emma Lazarus

This poem is found on the base of the Statue of Liberty. It was meant as a welcome to people coming to live in the United States from other lands.

Give me your tired,
    your poor,
Your huddled masses
    yearning to breathe free,
The wretched refuse of your
    teeming shore.
Send these, the homeless,
    tempest-tossed, to me:
I lift my lamp beside the
    golden door.

Monotone

By Carl Sandburg

The monotone of the rain is beautiful,
And the sudden rise and slow relapse
Of the long multitudinous rain.
The sun on the hills is beautiful,
Or a captured sunset sea-flung,
Bannered with fire and gold.
A face I know is beautiful—
With fire and gold of sky and sea,
And the peace of long warm rain.

Plowboy

By Carl Sandburg

After the last red sunset glimmer,
Black on the line of a low hill rise,
Formed into moving shadows, I saw
A plowboy and two horses lined against
   the gray,
Plowing in the dusk the last furrow.
The turf had a gleam of brown,
And smell of soil was in the air,
And, cool and moist, a haze of April.
I shall remember you long,
Plowboy and horses against the sky in
   shadow.
I shall remember you and the picture
You made for me,
Turning the turf in the dusk
And haze of an April gloaming.

This poem makes a wonderful monologue for a child to thoughtfully perform. It also has great potential for an activity in poetic visualization. Children can illustrate this picture in detail because of the descriptive nature of the poetry. A writing extension for this piece could be a child creating an illustration from present life and then writing a poem to describe the scene.

This Is the House That Jack Built

This is the house that Jack built.

This is the malt
That lay in the house that Jack built.

This is the rat
That ate the malt
That lay in the house that Jack built.

This is the cat
That killed the rat
That ate the malt
That lay in the house that Jack built.

This is the dog
That worried the cat
That killed the rat
That ate the malt
That lay in the house that Jack built.

This is the cow with the crumpled horn
That tossed the dog
That worried the cat
That killed the rat
That ate the malt
That lay in the house that Jack built.

This is maiden all forlorn
That milked the cow with the crumpled horn
That tossed the dog
That worried the cat
That killed the rat
That ate the malt
That lay in the house that Jack built.

This is the man all tattered and torn
That kissed the maiden all forlorn
That milked the cow with the crumpled horn
That tossed the dog
That worried the cat
That killed the rat
That ate the malt
That lay in the house that Jack built.

This Is the House That Jack Built *(cont.)*

This is the priest all shaven and shorn
That married the man all tattered and torn
That kissed the maiden all forlorn
That milked the cow with the crumpled horn
That tossed the dog
That worried the cat
That killed the rat
That ate the malt
That lay in the house that Jack built.

This is the cock that crowed in the morn
That waked the priest all shaven and shorn
That married the man all tattered and torn
That kissed the maiden all forlorn
That milked the cow with the crumpled horn
That tossed the dog
That worried the cat
That killed the rat
That ate the malt
That lay in the house that Jack built.

This is the farmer sowing his corn
That kept the cock that crowed in the morn
That waked the priest all shaven and shorn
That married the man all tattered and torn
That kissed the maiden all forlorn
That milked the cow with the crumpled horn
That tossed the dog
That worried the cat
That killed the rat
That ate the malt
That lay in the house that Jack built.

If I Can Stop One Heart From Breaking

By Emily Dickinson

If I can stop one heart from breaking,

I shall not live in vain;

If I can ease one life the aching,

Or cool one pain,

Or help one fainting robin

Unto his nest again,

I shall not live in vain.

Way Down South

Way down South where bananas grow,
A little ant stepped on an elephant's toe,
The elephant cried with tears in his eyes,
"Why don't you pick on someone your size?"

A horse and a flea and three blind mice
Sat on a curbstone shooting dice,
The horse he slipped and fell on the flea,
"Whoops," said the flea, "there's a horse on me!"

Way up North where there's ice and snow,
There lived a penguin and his name was Joe,
He got so tired of black and white,
He wore pink slacks to the dance last night!

Eli, Eli, he sells socks,
A dollar a pair, a nickel a box
The longer you wear them the shorter they get.
Throw'em in the water and they don't get wet.

Late last night, I had a real strange dream,
Ate a nine-pound marshmallow my mom gave me,
When I woke up, I knew somethin' was wrong,
I looked around and saw my pillow was gone.

Bed in Summer

By Robert Louis Stevenson

In winter I get up at night
And dress by yellow candle-light.
In summer, quite the other way,
I have to go to bed by day.

I have to go to bed and see
The birds still hopping on the tree,
Or hear the grown-up people's feet
Still going past me in the street.
And does it not seem hard to you,
When all the sky is clear and blue,

And I should like so much to play,
To have to go to bed by day?

The Bee

By Isaac Watts

How doth the little busy bee
Improve each shining hour,
And gather honey all the day
From every opening flower!
How skillfully she builds her cell!
How neat she spreads the wax!
And labors hard to store it well
With the sweet food she makes.
In works of labor or of skill,
I would be busy too;
For Satan finds some mischief still
For idle hands to do.
In books, or work, or healthful play,
Let my first years be passed,
That I may give for every day
Some good account at last.

The Crocodile

By Lewis Carroll

How doth the little crocodile
Improve his shining tail,
And pour the waters of the Nile
On every golden scale!

How cheerfully he seems to grin!
How neatly spread his claws,
And welcomes little fishes in
With gently smiling jaws!

Who Has Seen the Wind?

By Christina Rossetti

Who has seen the wind?
Neither I nor you:
But when the leaves hang trembling
The wind is passing through.

Who has seen the wind?
Neither you nor I:
But when the trees bow down their
    heads
The wind is passing by.

I Had a Little Puppy

I had a little puppy,

His name was Tiny Tim.

I put him in the bathtub, to see if he
could swim.

He drank up all the water; he ate a bar
of soap.

The next thing you know he had a
bubble in his throat.

In came the doctor, in came the nurse,

In came the lady with the alligator
purse.

Out went the doctor, out went the
nurse,

Out went the lady with the alligator
purse.

I kissed my puppy's doctor, I kissed my
puppy's nurse,

And then I paid the lady with the
alligator purse.

Trees

By Joyce Kilmer

I think that I shall never see

A poem lovely as a tree.

A tree whose hungry mouth is prest

Against the sweet earth's flowing breast;

A tree that looks at God all day,

And lifts her leafy arms to pray;

A tree that may in summer wear

A nest of robins in her hair;

Upon whose bosom snow has lain;

Who intimately lives with rain.

Poems are made by fools like me,

But only God can make a tree.

My Shadow

By Robert Louis Stevenson

I have a little shadow that goes in and out with me,
And what can be the use of him is more than I can see.
He is very, very like me from the heels up to the head;
And I see him jump before me, when I jump into my bed.

The funniest thing about him is the way he likes to grow—
Not at all like proper children, which is always very slow;
For he sometimes shoots up taller like an India-rubber ball,
And he sometimes gets so little that there's none of him at all.

He hasn't got a notion of how children ought to play,
And can only make a fool of me in every sort of way.
He stays so close beside me, he's a coward you can see;
I'd think shame to stick to nursie as that shadow sticks to me!

One morning, very early, before the sun was up,
I rose and found the shining dew on every buttercup;
But my lazy little shadow, like an arrant sleepy-head,
Had stayed at home behind me and was fast asleep in bed.

A School Cheer

Al-Veevo, Al-Vivo
Al-Veevo, Vivo, boom,
Boom get a rat trap,
Bigger than a cat trap,
Boom get another one,
Bigger than the other one,
Cannonball, Cannonball,
Sis, boom, bah,
Our School, Our School,
Rah, rah, rah.

Replace "Our School" with the name of your school.

There Was an Old Man with a Beard

By Edward Lear

There was an Old Man with a
    beard,

Who said, "It is just as I feared! —

Two Owls and a Hen, four Larks
    and a Wren,

Have all built their nests in my
    beard."

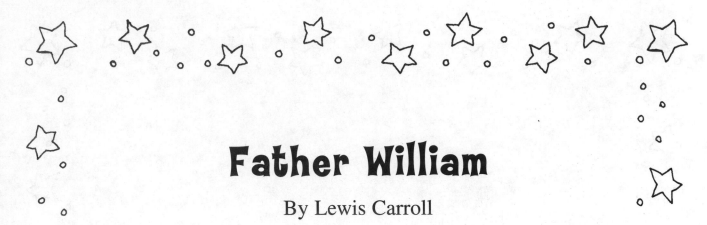

Father William

By Lewis Carroll

"You are old, father William," the young man said,
And your hair has become very white;
And yet you incessantly stand on your head—
Do you think, at your age, it is right?"
"In my youth," father William replied to his son,
"I feared it would injure the brain;
But now that I'm perfectly sure I have none,
Why, I do it again and again."

"You are old," said the youth, "as I mentioned before,
And have grown most uncommonly fat;
Yet you turned a back-somersault in at the door—
Pray, what is the reason of that?"
"In my youth," said the sage, as he shook his grey locks,
"I kept all my limbs very supple
By the use of this ointment—one shilling the box—
Allow me to sell you a couple."

Note: This poem is also available as a two-person Reader's Theater on page 111.

Father William *(cont.)*

"You are old," said the youth, "and your jaws are too weak
For anything tougher than suet;
Yet you finished the goose, with the bones and the beak—
Pray, how did you manage to do it?"
"In my youth," said his father, "I took to the law,
And argued each case with my wife;
And the muscular strength, which it gave to my jaw,
Has lasted the rest of my life."

"You are old," said the youth; "one would hardly suppose
That your eye was as steady as ever;
Yet you balanced an eel on the end of your nose—
What made you so awfully clever?"
"I have answered three questions, and that is enough,"
Said his father; "don't give yourself airs!
Do you think I can listen all day to such stuff?
Be off, or I'll kick you down stairs!"

Windy Nights

By Robert Louis Stevenson

Whenever the moon and stars are set,
Whenever the wind is high,
All night long in the dark and wet,
A man goes riding by.
Late in the night when the fires are out,
Why does he gallop and gallop about?
Whenever the trees are crying aloud,
And ships are tossed at sea,
By, on the highway, low and loud,
By at the gallop goes he.
By at the gallop he goes, and then
By he comes back at the gallop again.

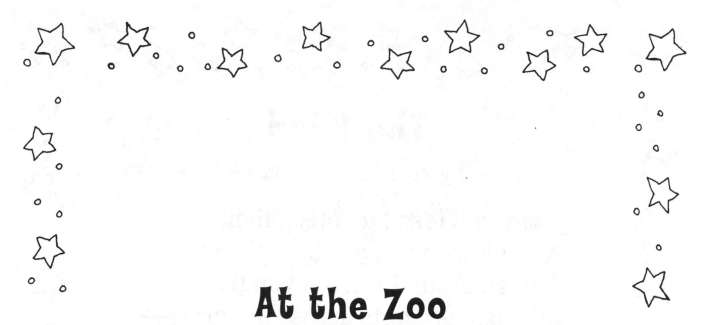

At the Zoo

By William Makepeace Thackeray

First I saw the white bear, then I saw the black;

Then I saw a camel with a hump upon his back;

Then I saw a grey wolf, with a mutton in his maw;

Then I saw a wombat waddle in the straw;

Then I saw the elephant a-waving of his trunk;

Then I saw the monkeys—mercy,

How unpleasantly they smelt.

The Wind

By Robert Louis Stevenson

I saw you toss the kites on high
And blow the birds about the sky;
And all around I heard you pass,
Like ladies' skirts across the grass—
O wind, a-blowing all day long,
O wind, that sings so loud a song!

I saw the different things you did,
But always you yourself you hid.
I felt you push, I heard you call,
I could not see yourself at all—
O wind, a-blowing all day long,
O wind, that sings so loud a song!

O you that are so strong and cold,
O blower, are you young or old?
Are you a beast of field and tree,
Or just a stronger child than me?
O wind, a-blowing all day long,
O wind, that sings so loud a song!

The Kid

By Walter Ben Hare

Suppose you was a kid like me,
And ma would take you on her knee
And fill the wash rag full of soap,
And hold you tight as any rope,
And wash yer eyes and nose and chin,
And 'hind your ears, and ever'thin',
And git some soap suds in yer eye,
And up yer nose, till you ist cry!
I bet you'd be as sore as me,
I bet you'd say worse words than "Gee!"
Now wouldn't you?

Suppose you was a kid, I say,
And got washed thirty times a day,
I bet you'd kick and holler, too,
And do things that you shouldn't do.
I bet you'd even cry and bawl,
For you don't have to wash at all!
And what's the use of it, I say?
You ist get dirty right away.
And then you have to wash some more!
I bet that it ud make you sore!
Now wouldn't it?

The Kid (cont.)

When I get growed and am a man
I'll wash on the installment plan.
And all my little girls and boys
Can play around with yells and noise,
And every day wade in the creek—
And only wash ist once a week!
And then, ist here—and here—and here!
[Points to forehead, cheeks and chin]
And wash with soap ist once a year!
Now if you was my little boy,
I bet you'd laugh and shout for joy!
Now wouldn't you?

34

Well Wishes

An Irish Toast

May there always be work for your
hands to do.

May your purse always hold a coin
or two.

May the sun always shine warm on
your windowpane.

May a rainbow be certain to follow
each rain.

A Polish Blessing

May the land be fertile beneath your feet.

May your days be gentle as the sun-
kissed dew.

May your hand be outstretched to all you
meet.

And may all men say "Brother or Sister"
when they speak of you.

The Night Before Christmas

By Clement Moore

A Poem for Two Voices

Voice One	Both	Voice Two
'Twas the night before Christmas, when all through the house		
Not a creature was stirring, not even a mouse;		
		The stockings were hung by the chimney with care,
		In hopes that St. Nicholas soon would be there.
The children were nestled all snug in their beds,		
While visions of sugarplums danced in their heads.		
		And mamma in her 'kerchief, and I in my cap,
		Had just settled down for a long winter's nap,
		When out on the lawn there arose such a clatter,
		I sprang from the bed to see what was the matter.

The Night Before Christmas *(cont.)*

Voice One	Both	Voice Two

Away to the window I
flew like a flash,

Tore open the shutters and
threw up the sash.

The moon on the breast
of the new-fallen snow

Gave the lustre of mid-day to
objects below,

When, what to my
wondering eyes should
appear,

But a miniature sleigh, and
eight tiny reindeer,

With a little old driver, so
lively and quick,

I knew in a moment it must
be St. Nick.

More rapid than eagles his
coursers they came,

And he whistled, and
shouted, and called them by
name:

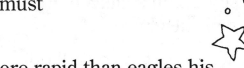

38

The Night Before Christmas *(cont.)*

Voice One	Both	Voice Two
"Now, Dasher!		
		now, Dancer!
Now, Prancer		
		and Vixen!
On, Comet!		
		on Cupid!
on, Donder		
		and Blitzen!
To the top of the porch!		
		to the top of the wall!
	Now dash away! dash away! dash away all!"	

As dry leaves that before the wild hurricane fly,

When they meet with an obstacle, mount to the sky,

So up to the house-top the coursers they flew,

With the sleigh full of toys, and St. Nicholas too.

The Night Before Christmas *(cont.)*

| Voice One | Both | Voice Two |

And then, in a twinkling, I heard on the roof

The prancing and pawing of each little hoof.

As I drew in my head, and was turning around,

Down the chimney St. Nicholas came with a bound.

He was dressed all in fur, from his head to his foot,

And his clothes were all tarnished with ashes and soot.

A bundle of toys he had flung on his back,

And he looked like a peddler just opening his pack.

His eyes—how they twinkled! his dimples how merry!

His cheeks were like roses, his nose like a cherry!

His droll little mouth was drawn up like a bow,

And the beard of his chin was as white as the snow.

The Night Before Christmas *(cont.)*

Voice One	**Both**	**Voice Two**

Voice One:

The stump of a pipe he
held tight in his teeth,

Voice Two:

And the smoke it
encircled his head
like a wreath.

Voice One:

He had a broad face and
a little round belly,

Voice Two:

That shook, when he
laughed, like a bowl full of
jelly.

Voice One:

He was chubby and plump,
a right jolly old elf,

Voice Two:

And I laughed when I saw
him, in spite of myself.

Voice One:

A wink of his eye and a
twist of his head

Voice Two:

Soon gave me to know I had
nothing to dread.

Both:

He spoke not a word, but
went straight to his work,

And filled all the
stockings; then turned
with a jerk,

And laying his finger
aside of his nose,

And giving a nod, up the
chimney he rose.

#10031 Texts for Fluency Practice—Level B

The Night Before Christmas *(cont.)*

Voice One	Both	Voice Two

He sprang to his sleigh,
to his team gave a whistle,

And away they all flew like
the down of a thistle.

But I heard him exclaim,
ere he drove out of sight,

"Happy Christmas to all,
And to all, a good night!"

Song Lyrics

The Erie Canal

I've got a mule,
Her name is Sal,
Fifteen years on the Erie Canal.
She's a good old worker
And a good old pal,
Fifteen years on the Erie Canal.

We've hauled some barges in our day
Filled with lumber, coal and hay
And ev'ry inch of the way I know
From Albany to Buffalo.
Low Bridge, ev'rybody down,

For it's Low Bridge,
We're coming to a town!
You can always tell your neighbor,
You can always tell your pal,
If you've ever navigated
On the Erie Canal.

The Animal Fair

I went to the Animal Fair
The birds and the beasts were there
The big baboon by the light of the moon
Was combing his auburn hair

The funniest was the monk
He sat on the elephant's trunk
The elephant sneezed and fell on his knees
And what became of the monk?
The monk, the monk, the monk?

I went to the Animal Fair
The birds and the beasts were there
The big baboon by the light of the moon
Was combing his auburn hair

You should have seen the monk
He sat on the elephant's trunk
The elephant sneezed and fell on his knees
And that was the end of the monk
The monk, the monk, the monk.

Home on the Range

Oh, give me a home, where the buffalo roam,
Where the deer and the antelope play,
Where seldom is heard a discouraging word,
And the skies are not cloudy all day.

Chorus:
Home, home on the range,
Where the deer and the antelope play,
Where seldom is heard a discouraging word,
And the skies are not cloudy all day.

Where the air is so pure, the zephyrs so free,
The breezes so balmy and light,
That I would not exchange my home on the range
For all of the cities so bright.

Chorus

Oh, give me a land where the bright diamond sand
Flows leisurely down the stream;
Where the graceful white swan goes gliding along
Like a maid in a heavenly dream.

Chorus

How often at night when the heavens are bright
With the light of the glittering stars,
Have I stood here amazed and asked as I gazed
If their glory exceeds that of ours.

Chorus

Yankee Doodle

Yankee Doodle went to town
A-riding on a pony
Stuck a feather in his hat
And called it macaroni.

Yankee Doodle, keep it up
Yankee Doodle dandy
Mind the music and the step
And with the girls be handy.

Father and I went down to camp
Along with Captain Gooding
And there we saw the men and boys
As thick as hasty pudding.

Yankee Doodle, keep it up
Yankee Doodle dandy
Mind the music and the step
And with the girls be handy

There was Captain Washington
Upon a slapping stallion
A-giving orders to his men
I guess there was a million.

Yankee Doodle, keep it up
Yankee Doodle dandy
Mind the music and the step
And with the girls be handy.

I'm a Yankee Doodle Dandy

By George M. Cohan

I'm a Yankee Doodle Dandy
A Yankee Doodle do or die!
A real-life nephew of my Uncle Sam,
Born on the Fourth of July.
I've got a Yankee Doodle sweetheart,
She's my Yankee Doodle joy.
Yankee Doodle went to London just to
     ride the ponies,
I am that Yankee Doodle boy.

Blow the Man Down

I'll sing you a song, a good song of the sea
With a way, hey, blow the man down.
And trust that you'll join in the chorus with me
Give me some time to blow the man down.
There was an old skipper I don't know his name
With a way, hey, blow the man down.
Although he once played a remarkable game
Give me some time to blow the man down.
His ship lay be-calmed in the tropical sea
With a way, hey, blow the man down.
He whistled all day but in vain for a breeze
Give me some time to blow the man down.

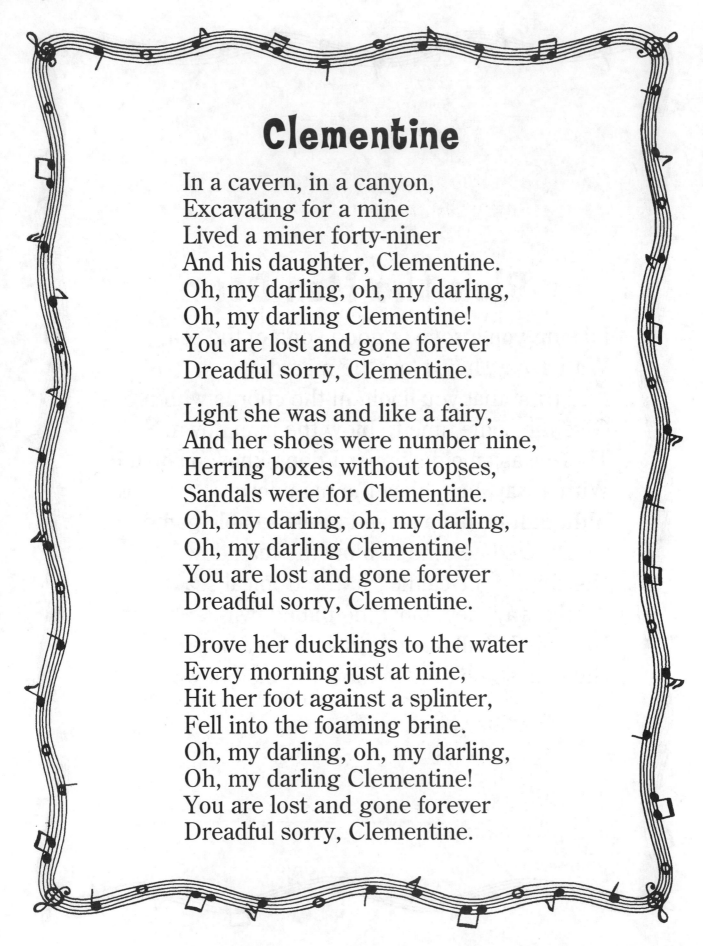

Clementine

In a cavern, in a canyon,
Excavating for a mine
Lived a miner forty-niner
And his daughter, Clementine.
Oh, my darling, oh, my darling,
Oh, my darling Clementine!
You are lost and gone forever
Dreadful sorry, Clementine.

Light she was and like a fairy,
And her shoes were number nine,
Herring boxes without topses,
Sandals were for Clementine.
Oh, my darling, oh, my darling,
Oh, my darling Clementine!
You are lost and gone forever
Dreadful sorry, Clementine.

Drove her ducklings to the water
Every morning just at nine,
Hit her foot against a splinter,
Fell into the foaming brine.
Oh, my darling, oh, my darling,
Oh, my darling Clementine!
You are lost and gone forever
Dreadful sorry, Clementine.

Clementine *(cont.)*

Ruby lips above the water,
Blowing bubbles soft and fine,
But alas, I was no swimmer,
So I lost my Clementine.
Oh, my darling, oh, my darling,
Oh, my darling Clementine!
You are lost and gone forever
Dreadful sorry, Clementine.

Then the miner, forty-niner
Soon began to peak and pine,
Thought he oughta join his daughter
Now he's with his Clementine.
Oh, my darling, oh, my darling,
Oh, my darling Clementine!
You are lost and gone forever
Dreadful sorry, Clementine.

There's a churchyard on the hillside
Where the flowers grow and twine.
There grow roses, 'mongst the posies
Fertilized by Clementine.
Oh, my darling, oh, my darling,
Oh, my darling Clementine!
You are lost and gone forever
Dreadful sorry, Clementine.

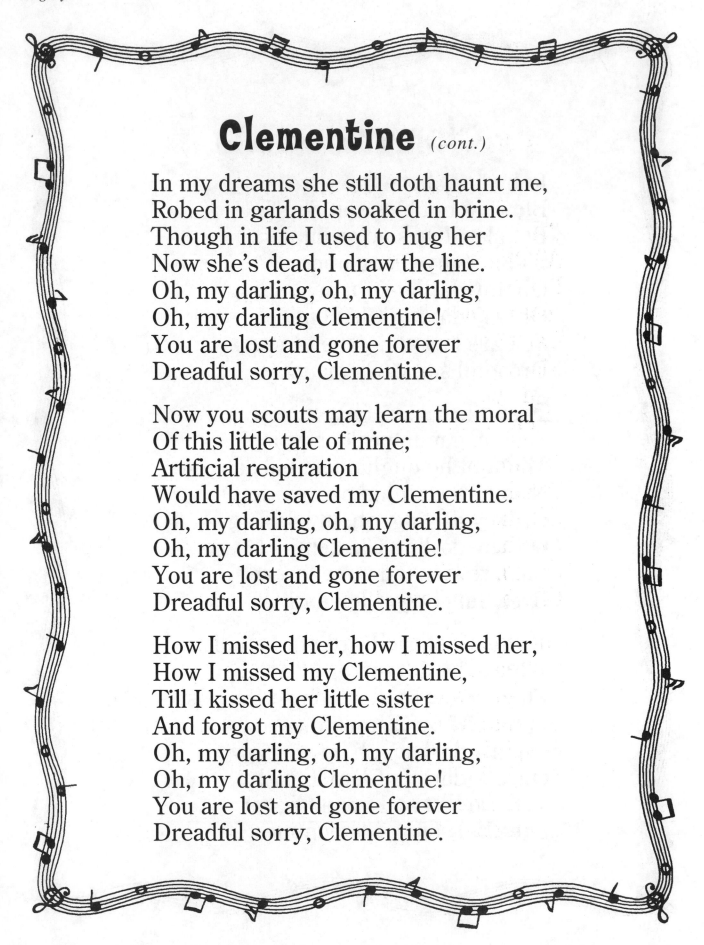

Clementine *(cont.)*

In my dreams she still doth haunt me,
Robed in garlands soaked in brine.
Though in life I used to hug her
Now she's dead, I draw the line.
Oh, my darling, oh, my darling,
Oh, my darling Clementine!
You are lost and gone forever
Dreadful sorry, Clementine.

Now you scouts may learn the moral
Of this little tale of mine;
Artificial respiration
Would have saved my Clementine.
Oh, my darling, oh, my darling,
Oh, my darling Clementine!
You are lost and gone forever
Dreadful sorry, Clementine.

How I missed her, how I missed her,
How I missed my Clementine,
Till I kissed her little sister
And forgot my Clementine.
Oh, my darling, oh, my darling,
Oh, my darling Clementine!
You are lost and gone forever
Dreadful sorry, Clementine.

52

I've Been Working on the Railroad

I've been working on the railroad
All the livelong day.
I've been working on the railroad
Just to pass the time away.
Can't you hear the whistle blowing
Rise up so early in the morn?
Can't you hear the captain shouting,
"Dinah, blow your horn"?

Dinah, won't you blow,
Dinah, won't you blow,
Dinah, won't you blow your horn?
Dinah, won't you blow,
Dinah, won't you blow,
Dinah, won't you blow your horn?

Someone's in the kitchen with Dinah.
Someone's in the kitchen, I know.
Someone's in the kitchen with Dinah,
Strumming on the old banjo, and singing
Fie, fi, fiddly i o,
Fie, fi, fiddly i o,
Fie, fi, fiddly i o,
Strumming on the old banjo.

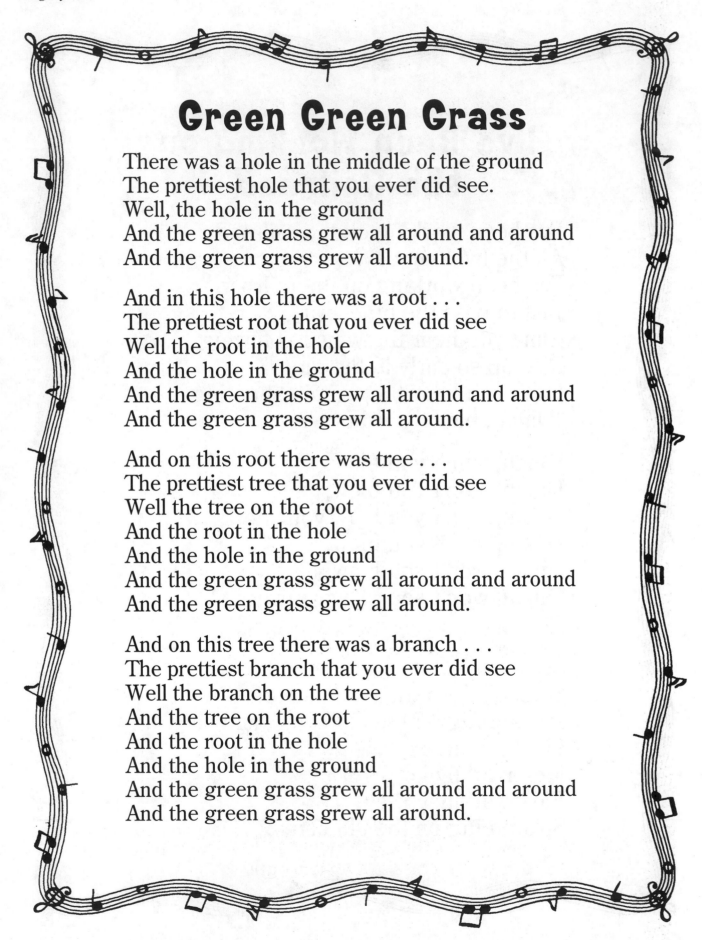

Green Green Grass

There was a hole in the middle of the ground
The prettiest hole that you ever did see.
Well, the hole in the ground
And the green grass grew all around and around
And the green grass grew all around.

And in this hole there was a root . . .
The prettiest root that you ever did see
Well the root in the hole
And the hole in the ground
And the green grass grew all around and around
And the green grass grew all around.

And on this root there was tree . . .
The prettiest tree that you ever did see
Well the tree on the root
And the root in the hole
And the hole in the ground
And the green grass grew all around and around
And the green grass grew all around.

And on this tree there was a branch . . .
The prettiest branch that you ever did see
Well the branch on the tree
And the tree on the root
And the root in the hole
And the hole in the ground
And the green grass grew all around and around
And the green grass grew all around.

Green Green Grass *(cont.)*

And on this branch there was twig . . .
The prettiest twig that you ever did see
Well the twig on the branch
And the branch on the tree
And the tree on the root
And the root in the hole
And the hole in the ground
And the green grass grew all around and around
And the green grass grew all around.

And on this twig there was a nest . . .
The prettiest nest that you ever did see
Well the nest on the twig
And the twig on the branch
And the branch on the tree
And the tree on the root
And the root in the hole
And the hole in the ground
And the green grass grew all around and around
And the green grass grew all around.
And in this nest there was an egg . . .
The prettiest egg that you ever did see
Well the egg in the nest
And the nest on the twig
And the twig on the branch
And the branch on the tree
And the tree on the root
And the root in the hole
And the hole in the ground
And the green grass grew all around and around
And the green grass grew all around.

Green Green Grass (cont.)

And in this egg there was a bird . . .
The prettiest bird that you ever did see
Well the bird on the egg
And the egg in the nest
And the nest on the twig
And the twig on the branch
And the branch on the tree
And the tree on the root
And the root in the hole
And the hole in the ground
And the green grass grew all around and around
And the green grass grew all around.

And on this bird there was a wing . . .
The prettiest wing that you ever did see
Well the wing on the bird
And the bird on the egg
And the egg in the nest
And the nest on the twig
And the twig on the branch
And the branch on the tree
And the tree on the root
And the root in the hole
And the hole in the ground
And the green grass grew all around and around
And the green grass grew all around.

56

Green Green Grass *(cont.)*

And on this wing, there was a feather . . .
The prettiest feather that you ever did see
Well the feather on the wing
And the wing on the bird
And the bird on the egg
And the egg in the nest
And the nest on the twig
And the twig on the branch
And the branch on the tree
And the tree on the root
And the root in the hole
And the hole in the ground
And the green grass grew all around and around
And the green grass grew all around.

Hush, Little Baby

Hush, little baby, don't say a word,
Mama's going to buy you a mockingbird.
And if that mockingbird don't sing,
Mama's going to buy you a diamond ring.
And if that diamond ring turns brass,
Mama's going to buy you a looking glass.
And if that looking glass gets broke,
Mama's going to buy you a billy goat.
And if that billy goat won't pull,
Mama's going to buy you a cart and bull.
And if that cart and bull turn over,
Mama's going to buy you a dog named Rover.
And if that dog named Rover won't bark,
Mama's going to buy you a horse and cart.
And if that horse and cart fall down,
You'll still be the sweetest little baby in town.

Oh, Susanna

I come from Alabama
With my banjo on my knee
I'm going to Louisiana,
My true love for to see
It rained all night
The day I left
The weather it was dry
The sun so hot,
I froze to death
Susanna, don't you cry

Oh, Susanna,
Oh don't you cry for me
For I come from Alabama
With my banjo on my knee

I had a dream the other night
When everything was still
I thought I saw Susanna
A-coming down the hill
The buckwheat cake
Was in her mouth
The tear was
In her eye
Says I, I'm coming from the south
Susanna, don't you cry

Oh, Susanna,
Oh don't you cry for me
For I come from Alabama
With my banjo on my knee

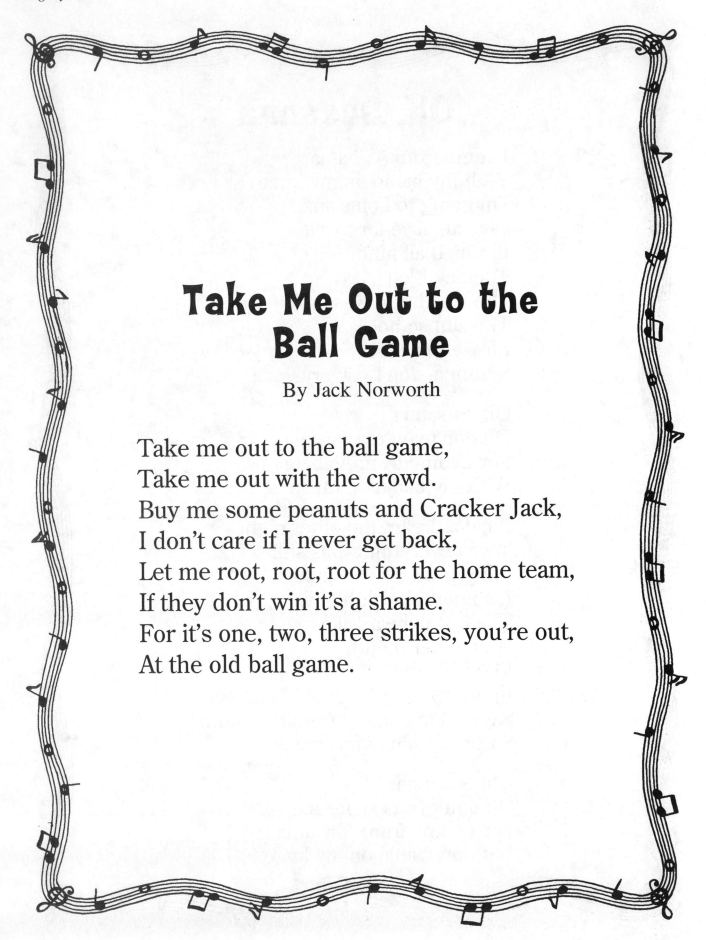

Take Me Out to the Ball Game

By Jack Norworth

Take me out to the ball game,
Take me out with the crowd.
Buy me some peanuts and Cracker Jack,
I don't care if I never get back,
Let me root, root, root for the home team,
If they don't win it's a shame.
For it's one, two, three strikes, you're out,
At the old ball game.

The Star-Spangled Banner

By Francis Scott Key

Oh, say, can you see, by the dawn's early light,
What so proudly we hail'd at the twilight's last
gleaming?
Whose broad stripes and bright stars, thro' the
perilous fight,
O'er the ramparts we watch'd, were so
gallantly streaming?
And the rockets' red glare, the bombs bursting
in air,
Gave proof thro' the night that our flag was
still there.
O say, does that star-spangled banner yet wave
O'er the land of the free and the home of the
brave?

America the Beautiful

By Katharine Lee Bates

O beautiful for spacious skies,
For amber waves of grain,
For purple mountain majesties
Above the fruited plain!

America! America!
God shed his grace on thee
And crown thy good with brotherhood
From sea to shining sea!

O beautiful for pilgrim feet
Whose stern impassion'd stress
A thoroughfare for freedom beat
Across the wilderness.

America! America!
God mend thine ev'ry flaw,
Confirm thy soul in self-control,
Thy liberty in law.

America the Beautiful *(cont.)*

O beautiful for heroes prov'd
In liberating strife,
Who more than self their country loved,
And mercy more than life.

America! America!
May God thy gold refine
Till all success be nobleness,
And ev'ry gain divine.

O beautiful for patriot dream
That sees beyond the years
Thine alabster cities gleam
Undimmed by human tears.

America! America!
God shed his grace on thee,
And crown thy good with brotherhood
From sea to shining sea.

A Bicycle Built for Two

Daisy, Daisy,

Give me your answer do!

I'm half crazy,

All for the love of you!

It won't be a stylish marriage,

I can't afford a carriage

But you'll look sweet upon the seat

Of a bicycle made for two.

The Sidewalks of New York

By Charles Lawlor and James W. Blake

East side, west side,
All around the town,
The tots sang "Ring-a-Rosie,"
"London Bridge is Falling Down."
Boys and girls together,
Me and Mamie O'Rourke,
Tripped the light fantastic,
On the sidewalks of New York.

You're a Grand Old Flag

By George M. Cohan

You're a grand old flag,
You're a high flying flag
And forever in peace may you wave.
You're the emblem of
The land I love.
The home of the free and the brave.
Ev'ry heart beats true
'neath the Red, White and Blue,
Where there's never a boast or brag.
Should auld acquaintance be forgot,
Keep your eye on the grand old flag.

My Bonnie Lies Over the Ocean

My Bonnie lies over the ocean,

My Bonnie lies over the sea.

My Bonnie lies over the ocean,

Please bring back my Bonnie to me.

Bring back,

Bring back,

Oh, bring back my Bonnie to me, to me.

Bring back,

Bring back,

Oh, bring back my Bonnie to me.

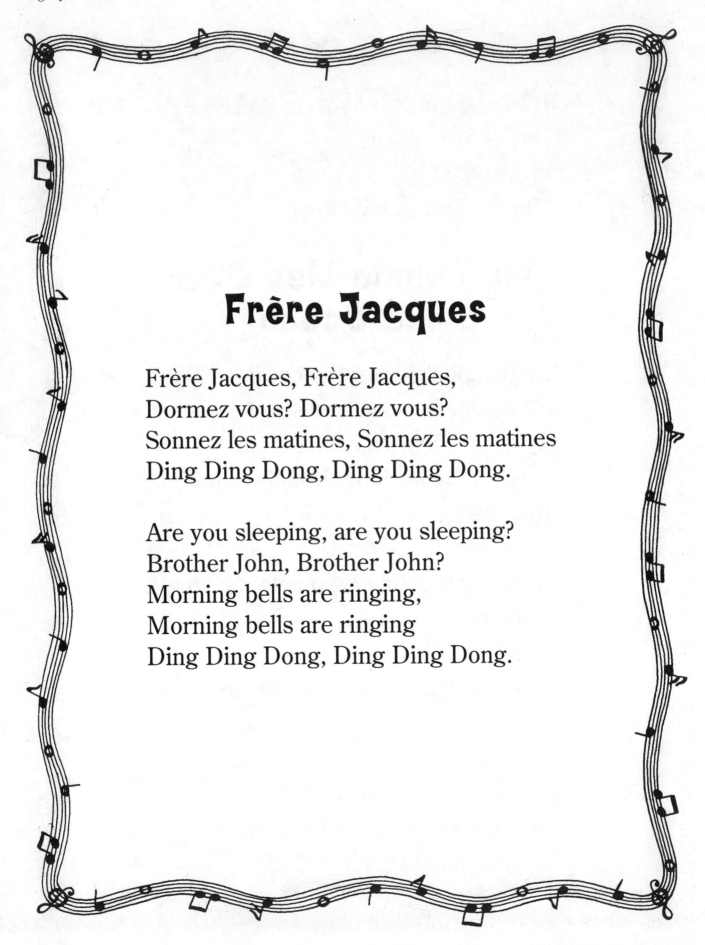

Frère Jacques

Frère Jacques, Frère Jacques,
Dormez vous? Dormez vous?
Sonnez les matines, Sonnez les matines
Ding Ding Dong, Ding Ding Dong.

Are you sleeping, are you sleeping?
Brother John, Brother John?
Morning bells are ringing,
Morning bells are ringing
Ding Ding Dong, Ding Ding Dong.

In the Good Old Summertime

By Ren Shields

There's a time in each year
That we always hold dear,
Good old summertime;
With the birds and the treeses
And sweet scented breezes,
Good old summertime,
When your day's work is over
Then you are in clover,
And life is one beautiful rhyme,
No trouble annoying,
Each one is enjoying,
The good old summertime.

In the good old summertime,
In the good old summertime,
Strolling through the shady lanes
With your baby mine.
You hold her hand
And she holds yours,
And that's a very good sign
That she's your tootsie-wootsie
In the good old summertime.

In the Good
Old Summertime *(cont.)*

To swim in the pool,
You'd play "hooky" from school,
Good old summertime;
You'd play "ringarosie"
With jim, kate and josie,
Good old summertime,
Those days full of pleasure
We now fondly treasure,
When we never thought it a crime,
To go stealing cherries,
With face brown as berries,
Good old summertime.

In the good old summertime,
In the good old summertime,
Strolling through the shady lanes
With your baby mine.
You hold her hand
And she holds yours,
And that's a very good sign
That she's your tootsie-wootsie
In the good old summertime.

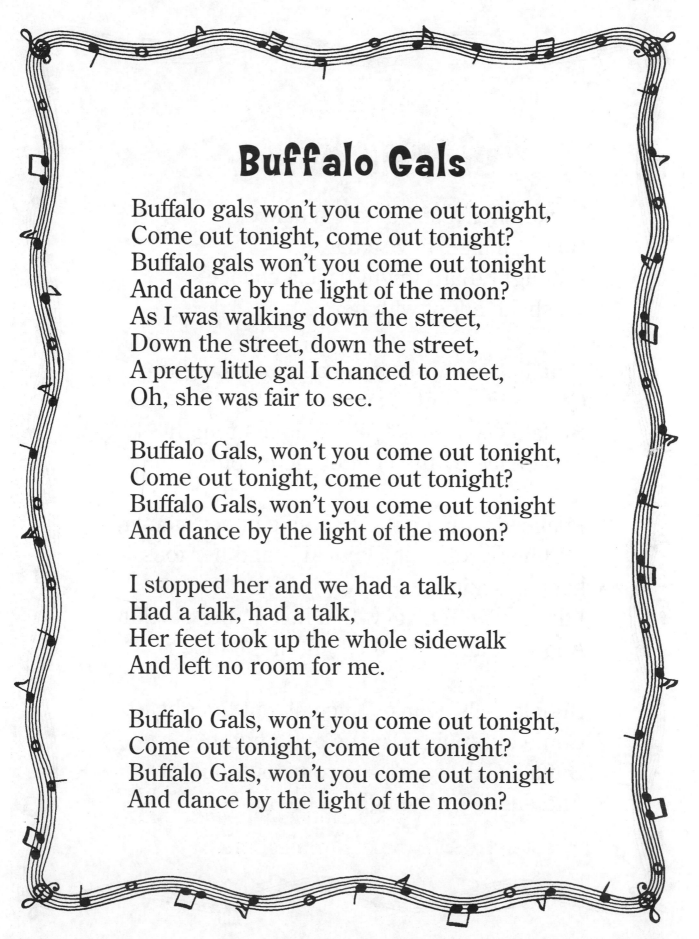

Buffalo Gals

Buffalo gals won't you come out tonight,
Come out tonight, come out tonight?
Buffalo gals won't you come out tonight
And dance by the light of the moon?
As I was walking down the street,
Down the street, down the street,
A pretty little gal I chanced to meet,
Oh, she was fair to see.

Buffalo Gals, won't you come out tonight,
Come out tonight, come out tonight?
Buffalo Gals, won't you come out tonight
And dance by the light of the moon?

I stopped her and we had a talk,
Had a talk, had a talk,
Her feet took up the whole sidewalk
And left no room for me.

Buffalo Gals, won't you come out tonight,
Come out tonight, come out tonight?
Buffalo Gals, won't you come out tonight
And dance by the light of the moon?

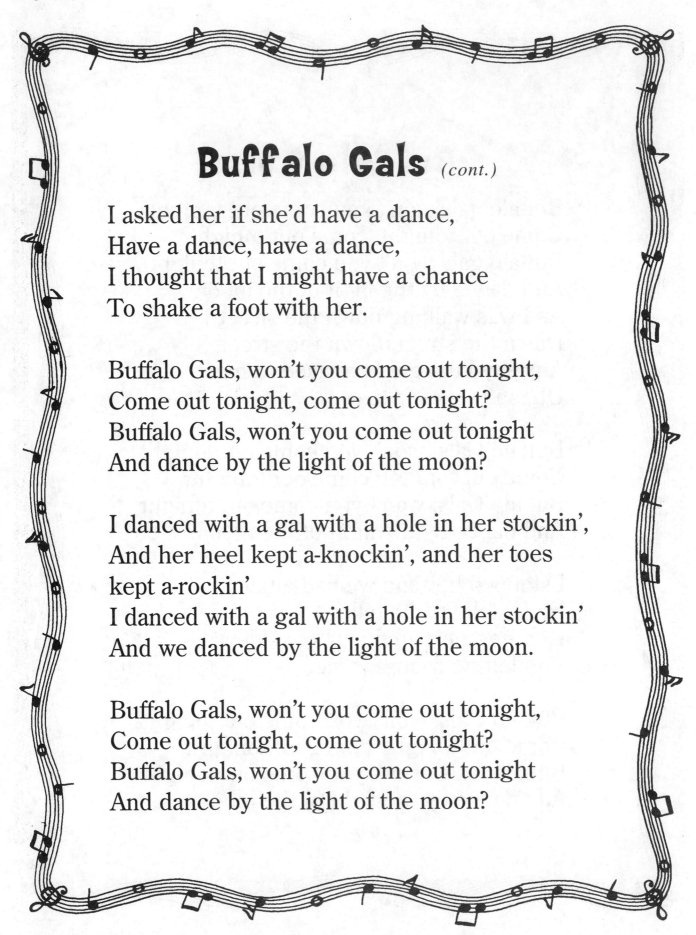

Buffalo Gals *(cont.)*

I asked her if she'd have a dance,
Have a dance, have a dance,
I thought that I might have a chance
To shake a foot with her.

Buffalo Gals, won't you come out tonight,
Come out tonight, come out tonight?
Buffalo Gals, won't you come out tonight
And dance by the light of the moon?

I danced with a gal with a hole in her stockin',
And her heel kept a-knockin', and her toes
kept a-rockin'
I danced with a gal with a hole in her stockin'
And we danced by the light of the moon.

Buffalo Gals, won't you come out tonight,
Come out tonight, come out tonight?
Buffalo Gals, won't you come out tonight
And dance by the light of the moon?

Tongue Twisters and Monologues

She Sells Sea Shells

She sells sea shells by the sea shore.

The shells she sells are surely seashells.

So if she sells shells on the seashore,

I'm sure she sells seashore shells.

A Tutor

A tutor who tooted a flute

Tried to tutor two tooters to toot.

Said the two to their tutor,

"Is it harder to toot

Or to tutor two tooters to toot?"

A Flea and a Fly

A flea and a fly flew up in a flue.

Said the flea, "Let us fly!"

Said the fly, "Let us flee!"

So they flew through a flaw in the flue.

Peter Piper

Peter Piper picked a peck of pickled peppers.

Did Peter Piper pick a peck of pickled peppers?

If Peter Piper picked a peck of pickled peppers,

Where's the peck of pickled peppers Peter Piper picked?

Betty Botter

By Mother Goose

Betty Botter bought some butter,

"But," she said, "the butter's bitter;

If I put it in my batter,

It will make my batter bitter;

But a bit of better butter,

That would make my batter better."

So she bought a bit of butter,

Better than her bitter butter,

And she put it in her batter,

And the batter was not bitter;

So 'twas better Betty Botter

Bought a bit of better butter.

When I Was a Boy

By Fred Rogers (Mr. Rogers)

When I was a boy, I used to think that strong meant having big muscles, great physical power; but the longer I live, the more I realize that real strength has much more to do with what is not seen. Real strength has to do with helping others.

The Milkmaid and Her Pail

I am Patty the Milkmaid. One morning I was going to market carrying my milk in a pail on my head. As I went along I began calculating what I would do with the money I would get for the milk.

"I'll buy some chickens from Farmer Brown," I thought to myself, "and they will lay eggs each morning, which I will sell to the parson's wife. With the money that I get from the sale of these eggs I'll buy myself a new fancy frock and a chip hat; and when I go to market, won't all the young men come up and speak to me! Polly Shaw will be that jealous; but I don't care. I shall just look at her and toss my head like this."

But as I spoke, disaster happened. As I tossed my head back, the pail fell off, and the milk spilled all over the ground.

I had to go home and tell my mother what had happened.

"Ah, my child," my mother said, "Do not count your chickens before they are hatched."

Dorothy and the Emerald City

From *The Wizard of Oz*, by Frank Baum.

Changed to first person by Lorraine Griffith

Even with eyes protected by my green spectacles, my friends and I were at first dazzled by the brilliancy of the wonderful city. The streets were lined with beautiful houses all built of green marble and studded everywhere with sparkling emeralds. We walked over a pavement of the same green marble, and where the blocks were joined together were rows of emeralds, set closely, and glittering in the brightness of the sun. The windowpanes were of green glass; even the sky above the city had a green tint, and the rays of the sun were green.

There were many people—men, women, and children— walking about, and these were all dressed in green clothes and had greenish skins. They looked at me and my strangely assorted company with wondering eyes, and the children all ran away and hid behind their mothers when they saw the Lion; but no one spoke to us. Many shops stood in the street, and I saw that everything in them was green. Green candy and green popcorn were offered for sale, as well as green shoes, green hats, and green clothes of all sorts. At one place a man was selling green lemonade, and when the children bought it I could see that they paid for it with green pennies.

There seemed to be no horses nor animals of any kind; the men carried things around in little green carts, which they pushed before them. Everyone seemed happy and contented and prosperous.

There's No Place Like Home

Written by L. Frank Baum (novel), Noel Langley, Florence Ryerson, and Edgar Allan Woolf

Dorothy, from the Wizard of Oz

But it wasn't a dream. It was a place. And you and you and you. . . and you were there. But you couldn't have been could you? No, Aunt Em, this was a real truly live place and I remember some of it wasn't very nice, but most of it was beautiful—but just the same all I kept saying to everybody was "I want to go home," and they sent me home! Doesn't anybody believe me? But anyway, Toto, we're home! Home. And this is my room, and you're all here and I'm not going to leave here ever, ever again. Because I love you all. And. . . Oh Auntie Em! There's no place like home!

Courage

Written by L. Frank Baum (novel), Noel Langley, Florence Ryerson, and Edgar Allan Woolf

The Lion from *The Wizard of Oz*

Courage!

What makes a king out of a slave?

Courage!

What makes the flag on the mast to wave?

Courage!

What makes the elephant charge his tusk,
In the misty mist or the dusky dusk?
What makes the muskrat guard his musk?

Courage!

What makes the sphinx the seventh wonder?

Courage!

What makes the dawn come up like thunder?

Courage!

What makes the Hottentot so hot?
What puts the "ape" in apricot?
What have they got that I ain't got?

Courage!

You can say that again!

Instead of a monologue, one voice could read the Lion's questions and a chorus could read the "Courage!" parts.

Good Evening, Audience

By Walter Ben Hare

Good evening, Mrs. Audience,
And Mr. Audience, too;
I hope you're glad to see me,
And will like me 'fore I'm through.
I'm here to bid you welcome,
I'm sure I like your style;
We'll soon become right friendly
If you will only smile.
I'll try to entertain you
With monologue and rhyme—
But if you won't assist me
We'll have a dreadful time.
The world is full of worry,
Let's forget it for a while,
And take a trip to Funland—
So stretch your mouth and smile.
Some speakers talk of trouble,
Of pessimistic creeds,
But just an S-M-I-L-E [spell]
Is all the old world needs.
Be gay, enthusiastic,
And cheerful all the while,
Forget your gloom and worries,
And smile, smile, smile!
And now the ice is broken,
We're friends, that's how it stands,
And if you feel as I do,
You'll tell me with your hands, [Pantomimes applause]
With song and jest and story,
I shall an hour beguile;
I'll do my best to please you,
If you'll smile, smile, smile!

#10031 Texts for Fluency Practice—Level B　　　84

Slugworth's Attempted Corruption

Written by Roald Dahl

Slugworth from *Charlie and the Chocolate Factory*

I congratulate you, little boy. Well done. You found the fifth Golden Ticket. May I introduce myself. Arthur Slugworth, President of Slugworth Chocolates, Incorporated. Now listen carefully because I'm going to make you very rich indeed. Mr. Wonka is at this moment working on a fantastic invention: the Everlasting Gobstopper. If he succeeds, he'll ruin me. So all I want you to do is to get hold of just one Everlasting Gobstopper and bring it to me so that I can find the secret formula. Your reward will be ten thousand of these. (he flips through a stack of money) Think it over, will you. A new house for your family, and good food and comfort for the rest of their lives. And don't forget the name: Everlasting Gobstopper.

If She Doesn't Scare You, No Evil Thing Will

Written by John Hughes, from the novel
by Dodie Smith

**Cruella De Vil from *101 Dalmations* speaking
to the dalmations**

You beasts! But I'm not beaten yet. You've won the battle, but I'm about to win the wardrobe. My spotty puppy coat is in plain sight and leaving tracks. In a moment I'll have what I came for, while all of you will end up as sausage meat, alone on some sad, plastic plate. Dead and medium red. No friends, no family, no pulse. Just slapped between two buns, smothered in onions, with fries on the side. Cruella De Vil has the last laugh!

The Boy Who Lived

Written by Steven Kloves,
from the novel by J.K. Rowling

Prof. Snape in *Harry Potter and the Sorcerer's Stone*

There will be no foolish wand-waving or silly incantations in this class. As such, I don't expect many of you to appreciate the subtle science and exact art that is potion making. However, for those of you who possess the pre-disposition, I can teach you how to bewitch the mind and ensnare the senses; I can tell you how to brew glory, bottle fame, and even put a stopper in death. Then again, maybe some of you have come to Hogwarts in possession of abilities so formidable that you feel comfortable enough to not pay attention. Mr. Potter, our new celebrity.

Angel Messages

Written by Richard LaGravenese & Elizabeth Chandler

Sara in *A Little Princess*

I don't have a mother either. . . she's in heaven with my baby sister. . . But that doesn't mean I can't talk to her, I talk to her all the time. . . I tell her everything and I know she hears me because. . . because that's what angels do. My mom is an angel and yours is too. With beautiful satin wings, a silk dress, and a crown of baby rosebuds, and they all live together in a castle. And do you know what it's made out of? Sunflowers. Hundreds of them, so bright they shine like the sun. And when they want to go anywhere they just whistle, like this. . .(whistles) and a cloud swoops down to the front gate and picks them up and as they ride through the air, over the moon and through the stars. . . until they are hovering right above us, that's how they can look down and make sure we're all right. And sometimes they even send messages. Of course you can't hear them with all the noise you were making. . . but don't worry they'll always try again. . . just in case you missed them.

Reader's Theater Scripts

Radio Warning

A Reader's Theater for two voices

Americans: Please divert your course 15 degrees to the north to avoid a collision.

Canadians: Recommend you divert YOUR course 15 degrees to the south to avoid a collision.

Americans: This is the captain of a US Navy ship. I say again, divert YOUR course.

Canadians: No, I say again divert YOUR course.

Americans: THIS IS THE AIRCRAFT CARRIER *USS ENTERPRISE*; WE ARE A LARGE WARSHIP OF THE US NAVY. DIVERT YOUR COURSE NOW.

Canadians: This is Rocky Point Lighthouse. Your call.

Shadow March

By Robert Louis Stevenson

A Reader's Theater for 4 voices

R1: All around the house is the

ALL: jet-black night;

R2: It stares through the window-pane;

R3: It crawls in the corners, hiding from the light,

R4: And it moves with the

ALL: moving flame.

R2: Now my little heart goes a beating like a drum,
With the breath of the Bogies in my hair;

R3: And all around the candle and the crooked shadows come,
And go marching along up the stair.

R1 & 2: The shadow of the balusters,

R3& 4: the shadow of the lamp,

R1: The shadow of the child that goes to bed.

R2: All the wicked shadows coming tramp,

R3& 4: tramp,

ALL: tramp,

R1: With the black night overhead.

R2: All around the house is the

ALL: jet-black night . . .

This is a Reader's Theater created from a poem by an author who must have been fascinated by shadows. "Shadow March" is a poem that could "scare the living daylights" out of you if someone was saying it mysteriously in the dark with just a flashlight glowing! Hey! What a great idea. . .

Reader's Theater

By Lorraine Griffith

A Reader's Theater for 5 voices

R1: My teacher just told me we were going to do something called, "Reader's Theater" this year!

R2–5: We LOVE IT!

R1: What is "Reader's Theater"?

R2: It's acting with your voice!

R3: It's telling a story without any props

R4: or costumes

R5: or scenery!

R1: Do you mean the story is like a movie in your mind?

R2–5: Yes! What a perfect description!

R2: And if the story is frightening, your voice is scary.

R3: If the story is amazing, your voice shows you are flabbergasted.

R1: Flabbergasted?

R2–5: FLABBERGASTED!

R2: We love to use fantastic words!

R4: But if the story is sad, your voice is heartbreaking.

R5: And if the story is happy, you sound thrilled to pieces!

R1: But how do you memorize all those lines in just one week?

R2: You don't! My teacher says, "Never memorize your lines because you will quit working on the meaning of the text!"

Reader's Theater *(cont.)*

R1: How do you practice then if you aren't memorizing the lines?

R3: On Mondays, we practice pro-nun-ci-a-tion!

R4: On Tuesdays, we make sure our parts have a flow, like a rolling river so people can hear the meaning . . .

R2: Instead of just a jumble of words.

R5: On Wednesdays, we work on making the words expressive!

R3: Wednesdays make us feel like movie stars, because we love to be dramatic!

R2: On Thursdays, we practice projecting our voices, making them loud enough so everyone in the audience can hear our lines.

R3: I've even learned to whisper loud enough for everyone to hear me in the back of the room.

R1: How do you practice saying your lines at the right time?

R3: Sometimes I practice with my mom or dad,

R4: but sometimes I just practice alone in front of the mirror in my bedroom.

R2–5: And then on Fridays, we perform!

R2& 4: Sometimes we read poetry,

R3& 5: Sometimes we read humorous stories,

R2: Sometimes we read non-fiction, informational selections.

R3–5: But we always have fun!

ALL: Because we LOVE Reader's Theater!

This is a script I use the first week of school, more to educate the parents than anything, because most of my students' practice is done at home. This script can be revised to suit any teacher's needs. Some teachers choose to do all of the Reader's Theater Scripts at school and would find this script unnecessary.

❊ The Velveteen Rabbit: Scene One ❊

For three voices: Narrator (N), Rabbit (R) , and Skin Horse (SH)

R: "What is REAL?"

N: asked the Rabbit one day, when they were lying side by side near the nursery fender, before Nana came to tidy the room.

R: "Does it mean having things that buzz inside you and a stick-out handle?"

SH: "Real isn't how you are made. It's a thing that happens to you. When a child loves you for a long, long time, not just to play with, but REALLY loves you, then you become Real."

R: "Does it hurt?"

SH: "Sometimes,"

N: The Skin Horse was always truthful. "When you are Real you don't mind being hurt."

R: "Does it happen all at once, like being wound up or bit by bit?"

SH: "It doesn't happen all at once. You become. It takes a long time. That's why it doesn't happen often to people who break easily, or have sharp edges, or who have to be carefully kept. Generally, by the time you are Real, most of your hair has been loved off, and your eyes drop out and you get loose in your joints and very shabby. But these things don't matter at all, because once you are Real you can't be ugly, except to people who don't understand."

R: "I suppose you are real?"

N: And then Rabbit wished he had not said it, for he thought the Skin Horse might be sensitive. But the Skin Horse only smiled.

SH: "The Boy's Uncle made me Real. That was a great many years ago; but once you are Real you can't become unreal again. It lasts for always."

N: The Rabbit sighed. He thought it would be a long time before this magic called Real happened to him. He longed to become Real, to know what it felt like; and yet the idea of growing shabby and losing his eyes and whiskers was rather sad. He wished that he could become it without these uncomfortable things happening to him.

This is a classic piece of literature introducing the whole idea of "being real." There are three different scenes in this collection. You will want the children to have read or heard the whole book of the Velveteen Rabbit so that they understand where the scene fits into the whole story.

The Velveteen Rabbit: Scene Two

For five voices: Narrator 1 (N1), Narrator 2 (N2), Narrator 3 (N3), Narrator 4 (N4), Boy (B)

R: "What is REAL?"

N1: There was a person called Nana who ruled the nursery.

N2: Sometimes she took no notice of the playthings lying about,

N3: and sometimes,

N2 & 4: for no reason whatever,

N1: she went swooping about like a great wind and hustled them away in cupboards. She called this (Nana Voice) "tidying up, tidying up!"

N2 & 3: and the playthings all hated it, especially the tin ones.

N2: The Rabbit didn't mind it so much, for wherever he was thrown he came down soft.

N3: One evening, when the Boy was going to bed, he couldn't find the china dog that always slept with him.

N1: Nana was in a hurry, and it was too much trouble to hunt for china dogs at bedtime, so she simply looked about her, and seeing that the toy cupboard stood open, she made a swoop.

N1: (Nana voice) "Here! Take your old Bunny! He'll do to sleep with you!"

N1: And she dragged the Rabbit out by one ear, and put him into the Boy's arms.

N2: That night,

N4: and for many nights after,

N2 & 3: the Velveteen Rabbit slept in the Boy's bed.

N4: At first he found it uncomfortable,

N2: for the Boy hugged him very tight, and sometimes he rolled over on him, and sometimes he pushed him so far under the pillow that the Rabbit could scarcely breathe.

N4: And he missed, too, those long moonlight hours in the nursery, when all the house was silent, and his talks with the Skin Horse.

The Velveteen Rabbit: Scene Two *(cont.)*

N3: But very soon he grew to like it, for the Boy used to talk to him, and made nice tunnels for him under the bedclothes that he said were like the burrow the real rabbits lived in.

N2 & 3: And they had splendid games together, in whispers, when Nana had gone away to her supper and left the night-light burning on the mantelpiece.

N4: And when the Boy dropped off to sleep, the Rabbit would snuggle down close under his little warm chin and dream, with the Boy's hands clasped close round him all night long.

N2: And so time went on, and the little Rabbit was very happy—so happy that he never noticed how his beautiful velveteen fur was getting shabbier and shabbier,

N3: and his tail becoming unsewn,

N4: and all the pink rubbed off his nose where the Boy had kissed him.

N1–4: Spring came, and they had long days in the garden, for wherever the Boy went the Rabbit went too.

N2: He had rides in the wheelbarrow,

N3: and picnics on the grass,

N4: and lovely fairy huts built for him under the raspberry canes behind the flower border.

N2: And once, when the Boy was called away suddenly to go to tea, the Rabbit was left out on the lawn until long after dusk,

N1: and Nana had to come and look for him with the candle because the Boy couldn't go to sleep unless he was there.

The Velveteen Rabbit: Scene Two *(cont.)*

N3: He was wet through with the dew and quite earthy from diving into the burrows the Boy had made for him in the flower bed,

N1: and Nana grumbled as she rubbed him off with a corner of her apron.

N1: (Nana voice) "You must have your old Bunny! Fancy all that fuss for a toy!"

B: "Give me my Bunny! You mustn't say that. He isn't a toy. He's REAL!"

N2: When the little Rabbit heard that he was happy, for he knew what the Skin Horse had said was true at last.

N3: The nursery magic had happened to him,

N4: and he was a toy no longer.

N2, 3, 4: He was Real.

N2: The Boy himself had said it.

N3: That night he was almost too happy to sleep, and so much love stirred in his little sawdust heart that it almost burst.

N4: And into his boot-button eyes, that had long ago lost their polish, there came a look of wisdom and beauty,

N1: so that even Nana noticed it next morning when she picked him up, and said, (Nana voice) "I declare if that old Bunny hasn't got quite a knowing expression!"

All: That was a wonderful summer!

This is a classic piece of literature describing the process of the velveteen rabbit actually "becoming real." There are three different scenes in this collection. You will want the children to have read or heard the whole book of The Velveteen Rabbit *so that they understand where the scene fits into the whole story.*

The Velveteen Rabbit: Scene Three

For six vocies: Narrator 1 (N1), Narrator 2 (N2), Narrator 3 (N3), Rabbit (R), Furry Rabbit (FR), Wild Rabbit (WR)

N1: Near the house where they lived there was a wood, and in the long June evening the Boy liked to go there after tea to play.

N2: He took the Velveteen Rabbit with him, and before he wandered off to pick flowers,

N3: or play at brigands among the trees,

N2: he always made the Rabbit a little nest somewhere among the bracken, where he would be quite cozy.

N3: For he was a kind-hearted little boy and he liked Bunny to be comfortable.

N1: One evening, while the Rabbit was lying there alone, watching the ants that ran to and fro between his velvet paws in the grass, he saw two strange beings creep out of the tall bracken near him.

N2: They were rabbits like himself, but quite furry and brand-new.

R: They must have been very well made, for their seams didn't show at all, and they changed shape in a strange way when they moved; one minute they were long and thin and the next minute fat and bunchy, instead of always staying the same like he did. Their feet padded softly on the ground,

N3: and they crept quite close to him, twitching their noses, while the Rabbit stared hard to see which side the clockwork stuck out, for he knew that people who jump generally have something to wind them up. But he couldn't see it. They were evidently a new kind of rabbit altogether.

The Velveteen Rabbit: Scene Three *(cont.)*

N2: They stared at him, and the little Rabbit stared back.

N1, 2, 3: And all the time their noses twitched.

FR: "Why don't you get up and play with us?"

R: "I don't feel like it,"

N2: Rabbit didn't want to explain that he had no clockwork.

FR: "Ho! It's as easy as anything,"

N3: And he gave a big hop sideways and stood on his hind legs.

FR: "I don't believe you can!"

R: "I can! I can jump higher than anything."

N1: He meant when the Boy threw him, but of course he didn't want to say so.

FR: "Can you hop on your hind legs?"

N2: That was a dreadful question, for the Velveteen Rabbit had no hind legs at all! The back of him was made all in one piece, like a pincushion. He sat still in the bracken, and hoped that the other rabbit wouldn't notice.

R: "I don't want to!"

N1: But the wild rabbits have very sharp eyes. And this one stretched out his neck and looked.

WR: "He hasn't got any hind legs. Fancy a rabbit without any hind legs."

N2: And he began to laugh.

R: "I have! I have got hind legs! I am sitting on them."

WR: Then stretch them out and show me, like this!"

N3: And he began to whirl around and dance, till the little Rabbit got quite dizzy.

R: "I don't like dancing. I'd rather sit still!"

N1: But all the while he was longing to dance, for a funny new tickly feeling ran through him, and he felt he would give anything in the world to be able to jump about like these rabbits did.

The Velveteen Rabbit: Scene Three *(cont.)*

N2: The strange rabbit stopped dancing, and came quite close.

N3: He came so close this time that his long whiskers brushed the Velveteen Rabbit's ear,

N1: and then he wrinkled his nose suddenly and flattened his ears and jumped backwards.

WR: "He doesn't smell right! He isn't a rabbit at all! He isn't real!"

R: "I am Real! I am Real! The Boy said so!"

N2: And he nearly began to cry.

N3: Just then there was a sound of footsteps, and the Boy ran past near them,

N2: and with a stamp of feet and a flash of white tails the two strange rabbits disappeared.

R: "Come back and play with me! Oh, do come back! I know I am Real!"

N1: But there was no answer, only the little ants ran to and fro, and the bracken swayed gently where the two strangers had passed.

N1, 2, 3: The Velveteen Rabbit was all alone.

R: "Oh, dear! Why did they run away like that? Why couldn't they stop and talk to me?"

N1: For a long time he lay very still, watching the bracken, and hoping that they would come back.

N2: But they never returned, and presently the sun sank lower and the little white moths fluttered out,

N3: and the Boy came and carried him home.

This is a classic piece of literature showing the difference between "being real" because you are loved and actually being a "real" bunny. There are three different scenes in this collection. You will want the children to have read or heard the whole book of the Velveteen Rabbit *so that they understand where the scene fits into the whole story.*

The River Bank

A selection from *The Wind in the Willows*, by Kenneth Grahame

For five voices: Narrators 1–4 (N1), (N2), (N3), (N4) and Mole

N1: The Mole had been working very hard all the morning, spring-cleaning his little home.

N2: First with brooms,

N3: then with dusters;

N4: then on ladders and steps and chairs,

N3: with a brush and a pail of whitewash;

N2: till he had dust in his throat and eyes,

N1: and splashes of whitewash all over his black fur,

N2: and an aching back and weary arms.

N1: Spring was moving in the air above

N1 & 2: and in the earth below

N1, 2, 3: and around him,

N4: penetrating even his dark and lowly little house with its spirit of divine discontent and longing.

N1: It was small wonder, then, that he suddenly flung down his brush on the floor, and said

Mole: 'Bother!'

ALL: and

Mole: 'O blow!'

ALL: and also

Mole: 'Hang spring-cleaning!'

ALL: and bolted out of the house without even waiting to put on his coat.

The River Bank *(cont.)*

N2: Something up above was calling him imperiously,

N3: and he made for the steep little tunnel which answered in his case to the graveled carriage-drive owned by animals whose residences are nearer to the sun and air.

N4: So he scraped

N3: and scratched

N2: and scrabbled

N3: and scrooged

N4: and then he scrooged again

N3: and scrabbled

N2: and scratched

N4: and scraped,

N2: working busily with his little paws and muttering to himself,

Mole: 'Up we go! Up we go!'

N3: till at last,

N1, 2, 3, 4: POP! (with your finger in your mouth)

N4: his snout came out into the sunlight,

N1: and he found himself rolling in the warm grass of a great meadow.

Our class had some discussions on the author's craft of alliteration with the "scraped, scratched, scrabbled, scrooged, scrabbled, scratched, and scraped" section of this script. Having read The Wind and the Willows *will help your students enjoy the character's rendition of spring cleaning a mole hole.*

The Real McCoy

By Lorraine Griffith

For five voices

R1: Hey! Take a look at my new science fiction *Star Wars* book!

R2 & 5: Are you sure it's the real McCoy?

R1, 3, 4: Pardon me?

R3: Hey! Take a peek at my new skateboard, fast and sleek!

R2 & 5: Are you sure it's the real McCoy?

R1, 3, 4: Pardon me?

R4: Hey! Take a gander at my new yellow-spotted salamander!

R2 & 5: Are you sure it's the real McCoy?

R1, 3, 4: Excuse me?

R1: Why do you keep saying that? "Are you sure it's the real McCoy?"

R2: Well, we're doing a report on a famous African American inventor.

R5: Elijah McCoy was born in 1844 to fugitive slaves residing in Canada.

R2: McCoy was trained in Scotland as a mechanical engineer.

R5: He moved to Michigan after the Civil War. Discrimination kept him from practicing his trade as a mechanical engineer, so he worked as a fireman on the Michigan Central Railroad.

R2: There was a problem with the trains. They had to stop the train often simply to oil the locomotive.

R5: Elijah McCoy invented the first automatic lubricating cup to oil the locomotive while the train was in motion.

R1, 3, 4: The first automatic lubricating cup? And the train was in motion? WOW!

R2: Eventually he began a manufacturing company to produce the automatic lubricating cups. When this invention spread to other manufacturers, there were copies made of his cup.

R5: Customers who wanted to be sure about the quality of their purchase, would ask if the cup was the "real McCoy."

R1, 3, 4: Okay! We get it now!!

R1: My *Star Wars* book,

R3: My skateboard,

R4: And my yellow-spotted salamander

R1, 3, 4: Are all "the real McCoys"!

This is a script best staged with readers 2 & 5 on one side and readers 1, 3, & 4 on the other. Looking into the origin of sayings and phrases is a good way to study important events in history and culture. Until I researched this script, I didn't realize the saying related to the famous inventor.

My Shadow

By Robert Louis Stevenson

For four voices

Reader 1: I have a little shadow that goes in and out with me,

Reader 2: And what can be the use of him is more then I can see.

Reader 1: He is very, very like me from the heels up to the head;

Reader 2: And I see him jump before me when I jump into my bed.

Reader 3: The funniest thing about him is the way he likes to grow,

Reader 4: Not at all like proper children, which is always very slow;

Reader 3: For sometimes he shoots up taller like an Indian rubber ball,

Reader 4: And he sometimes gets so little that there is none of him at all.

Reader 1: He hasn't got a notion of how children ought to play,

Reader 2: And can only make a fool of me in every sort of way.

Reader 1: He stays so close behind me he's a coward you can see;

Reader 2: I'd think shame to stick to nursie as that shadow sticks to me!

Reader 3: One morning, very early before the sun was up,

Reader 4: I rose and found the shining dew on every buttercup;

Reader 3: But my lazy little shadow like an arrant sleepy-head,

Reader 4: had stayed at home behind me and was fast asleep in bed.

Little Orphant Annie

For five voices: Readers 1, 2, 3, and 4, and Annie

R1: James Whitcomb Riley wrote an inscription at the beginning of this poem, Inscribed with all faith and affection

To all the little children:

R2: —The happy ones;

R3: And sad ones;

R4: The sober and the silent ones;

R2: The boisterous and glad ones;

R4: The good ones — Yes, the good ones, too;

All: And all the lovely bad ones.

R1: Now here is the poem — Little Orphant Annie

R3: Little Orphant Annie's come to our house to stay,
An' wash the cups an' saucers up,
An' brush the crumbs away,

R4: An' shoo the chickens off the porch,
An' dust the hearth, an' sweep,

R2: An' make the fire,
An' bake the bread,
An' earn her board-an-keep;

R1: An' all us other childern, when the supper-things is done,
We set around the kitchen fire an' has the mostest fun,
A-listenin' to the witch-tales 'at Annie tells about,

All: An' the Gobble-uns 'at gits you
Ef you
Don't
Watch
Out!

Annie: Wunst they wuz a little boy wouldn't say his prayers, —
An' when he went to bed at night, away up-stairs,
His Mammy heerd him holler, an' his Daddy heerd him bawl,
An' when they turn't the kivvers down, he wuzn't there at all!
An' they seeked him in the rafter-room, an' cubby-hole, an' press,
An seeked him up the chimbly-flue, an' ever'-wheres, I guess;
But all they ever found wuz thist his pants an' roundabout: —

Little Orphant Annie *(cont.)*

All: An' the Gobble-uns 'll git you
Ef you
Don't
Watch
Out!

Annie: An' one time a little girl 'ud allus laugh an' grin,
An' make fun of ever' one, an' all her blood-an'-kin;
An' wunst, when they was "company," an' ole folks wuz there,
She mocked 'em an' shocked 'em, an' said she didn't care!
An' thist as she kicked her heels, an' turn't to run an' hide,
They wuz two great big Black Things a-standin' by her side,
An' they snatched her through the ceilin' 'for she knowed what she's about!

All: An' the Gobble-uns 'll git you
Ef you
Don't
Watch
Out!

R1: An' little Orphant Annie says, when the blaze is blue,

R2: An' the lamp-wick sputters, an' the wind goes woo-oo!

R3: An' you hear the crickets quit, an' the moon is gray,

R4: An' the lightnin' bugs in dew is all squenched away, —

Annie: You better mind yer parunts, an' yer teachurs fond an' dear,
An' cherish them 'at loves you, an' dry the orphant's tear,
An' he'p the pore an' needy ones 'at clusters all about,

All: Er the Gobble-uns 'll git you
Ef you
Don't
Watch
Out!

This is one of those scripts that has a dialect, much like "When the Frost is on the Punkin." Annie needs to be able to be pretty scary, leaning forward into the audience as she tells her stories. The whole group will be more effective if they use a gravelly, campfire whisper on the repeated "Gobble-uns 'll git you" part. My students had Annie stand in the center and the four readers looked at her in wonder and horror as she told her stories.

Chicago Poet

By Carl Sandburg

A Reader's Theater for two voices

R1: I saluted a nobody.
I saw him in a looking-glass.
He smiled—

R2: So did I.

R1: He crumpled the skin on his forehead, frowning—

R2: So did I.

R1: Everything I did he did.

R2: I said "Hello, I know you."
And I was a liar to say so.

R1: Ah, this looking-glass man!

R2: Liar,

R1: Fool,

R2: Dreamer,

R1: Play-actor,

R2: Soldier

R1: Dusty drinker of dust—

R2: Ah!

R1: He will go with me
Down the dark stairway
When nobody else is looking,
When everybody else is gone.

R2: He locks his elbow in mine,
I lose all—

Both: But not him.

This script is effectively performed with the two speakers facing one another a bit at an angle as if looking into a mirror. If facial expressions were mimicked as the text implies, it would add to the audience's perception of what is happening in the poem.

The Bear and the Two Travelers

For three voices: Narrator, Man 1, and Man 2

Narrator: This is a fable of two men who were traveling together, walking through the woods on their way to a final destination. Suddenly a bear appeared before them on their path and frightened the men.

Man 1: I didn't think twice, climbing quickly into a tree to save myself by hiding in the branches.

Man 2: I followed my fellow traveler, but tripped. Knowing that I would soon be attacked, I remained on the ground, motionless.

Man 1: From my safe spot I watched the bear as he felt the man lying on the ground with his snout, smelling him and nuzzling him all over.

Man 2: I held my breath, and pretended to be dead.

Narrator: The bear soon left, for it is said a bear will not touch a dead body. When the bear was definitely gone, the other Traveler descended from the tree, and jokingly asked his friend a question.

Man 1: What was it the Bear whispered in your ear?

Man 2: He gave me this advice: never travel with a friend who deserts you at the approach of danger.

Narrator: The moral of this fable is:

ALL: Misfortune tests the sincerity of friends.

Cal Ripken

By Lorraine Griffith

For 4 readers

R1: Cal Ripken is known as the Iron Man of baseball.

R2: On September 6, 1995, he surpassed the standing record for most games played consecutively.

R3: A ten minute standing ovation by an ecstatic crowd was followed with the following speech:

Cal: Tonight I want to make sure you know how I feel. As I grew up here, I not only had dreams of being a big-league ballplayer, but also of being a Baltimore Oriole. As a boy and a fan, I know how passionate we feel about baseball and the Orioles here. And as a player, I have benefited from this passion.

R1: Cal Ripkin was born in Maryland on August 24th, 1960.

R2: Following graduation from Aberdeen High School, he was drafted by the Orioles' minor league team.

R3: He played for them until he began the big leagues at the age of 21.

Cal: For all of your support over the years, I want to thank you, the fans of Baltimore, from the bottom of my heart. This is the greatest place to play. This year has been unbelievable. I've been cheered in ballparks all over the country. People not only showed me their kindness, but more importantly, they demonstrated their love of the game of baseball. I give my thanks to baseball fans everywhere. . . Tonight, I stand here, overwhelmed, as my name is linked with the great and courageous Lou Gehrig. I'm truly humbled to have our names spoken in the same breath.

R1: Let me tell you a little about Lou Gehrig. He was born in June of 1903 in New York City.

R2: He was also a tremendously talented ball player, a teammate of Babe Ruth's, known for his hard work at the game of baseball.

R3: Up until this point, Gehrig had held the record for most consecutive games played: 2,130 games.

Cal Ripken *(cont.)*

Cal: Some may think our greatest connection is because we both played many consecutive games. Yet, I believe in my heart that our true link is a common motivation — a love of the game of baseball, a passion for our team, and a desire to compete on the very highest level.

R1: Both Lou Gehrig and Cal Ripkin were know for their excellence, dependability, and consistency. They were responsible human beings who showed the world dependability through baseball.

R2: Gehrig played through a broken thumb, a broken toe, and back sprains, never missing a game in thirteen years.

R3: When he played his last game, he was dying of a disease later named "Lou Gehrig's Disease." His early death made him a legend admired throughout baseball history.

Cal: I know that if Lou Gehrig is looking on tonight's activities, he isn't concerned about someone playing one more consecutive game than he did. Instead, he's viewing tonight as just another example of what is good and right about the great American game. Whether your name is Gehrig or Ripken, DiMaggio, or Robinson, or that of some youngster who picks up his bat or puts on his glove, you are challenged by the game of baseball to do your very best day in and day out. And that's all I've tried to do.

R1: Cal Ripken retired from baseball on October 6, 2001.

R2: He holds the record for the most consecutive games played, 2,632.

R3: Cal Ripken will be known forever as the Iron Man of baseball, a man of dependable character.

I used this script for character education during our month-long unit on responsibility. A performance is more effective when Cal Ripken stands off to the side and the narrators stand together in another area. You may even want to have Cal wear a baseball jersey or cap.

Father William

By Lewis Carroll

A poem for two voices

V1: "You are old, father William," the young man said,
"And your hair has become very white;
And yet you incessantly stand on your head—
Do you think, at your age, it is right?"

V2: "In my youth," father William replied to his son,
"I feared it would injure the brain;
But now that I'm perfectly sure I have none,
Why, I do it again and again."

V1: "You are old," said the youth, "as I mentioned before,
And have grown most uncommonly fat;
Yet you turned a back-somersault in at the door—
Pray, what is the reason of that?"

V2: "In my youth," said the sage, as he shook his grey locks,
"I kept all my limbs very supple
By the use of this ointment—one shilling the box—
Allow me to sell you a couple."

Index